Clear, Heal and Strengthen

Your Energy Centers

by

Kelly Wallace

Professional Psychic Counselor

PsychicReadingsByDrKelly.webs.com[1]

©2010, 2013, 2017 All Right Reserved

Intuitive Living Publishing

---

1. http://PsychicReadingsByDrKelly.webs.com

Books By Kelly Wallace

-NONFICTION

10 Minutes A Day To A Powerful New Life

Become Your Higher Self

Chakras – Heal, Clear, And Strengthen Your Energy Centers

Clear Your Karma – The Healing Power Of Your Past Lives

Contacting And Working With Your Angels

Contacting And Working With Your Spirit Guides

Creating A Charmed Life – Enchantments to Attract, Repel, Cleanse & Heal

Energy Work – Heal, Cleanse, and Strengthen Your Aura

Finding Love – Ask Your Angels

Healing The Child Within

How To Cure Candida

Intuitive Living – Developing Your Psychic Gifts

Intuitive Tarot – Learn The Tarot Instantly

Is He The One? Finding And Keeping Your Soulmate

Leaving Love – Ask Your Angels

Make Miracles Happen

Master The Art Of Attracting Women

Master The Art Of Sex and Seduction

Messages From Your Angels

No-Sweat Homeschooling

Psychic Vampires – Protect Yourself From Energy Predators

Reprogram Your Subconscious – Get Everything You Want

Reprogram Your Subconscious For Financial Success

Soul Searching Soul Found – Increasing Your Spiritual Energy

The Art Of Happiness – Living A Life Of Peace And Meaning

Upgrade Your Life – Small Changes = Big Success

-Fiction - Sensual Romances

Best Friends Better Lovers

Bound To The Night

Confessions – Everyone Has A Secret At Ryder Ranch

Constant Craving

Cowboys Make Better Lovers

Gone And Back – Bad Boys Gone Good

Hard As Steele

Hellraiser

Invisible Evidence

Looking For Mr. Right

Love Immortal

Of Passion And Parsecs

One Wicket Night

Passionate Promises

Phantom Lover

The Chosen One

Two In The Bush

About Kelly Wallace

KELLY IS A BESTSELLING spiritual and self-help author, former radio show host, and has been a professional psychic counselor for over twenty years. She can see, hear, sense, and feel information sent from Spirit, the Universe, and a client's Higher Self.

Whether your problems or concerns center on love, finances, family, career, health, education, or your purpose in life, she writes books that will help you easily make lasting changes.

Kelly also offers professional psychic counseling[1], caring guidance, and solutions that work! More than just a typical psychic reading or counseling session, you will feel you've found a real friend during your time of need—whether you simply want answers and guidance to your current worries or concerns, or you're

---

1. http://psychicreadingsbydrkelly.webs.com/psychic-readings

interested in learning more about your soulmate, spirit guides, angels, past lives, or anything else.

Contact her today for an in-depth and life-altering reading!

Website: PsychicReadingsByDrKelly.webs.com[2]

Email: Dr.Kelly.Psychic.Counselor@gmail.com

---

2. http://psychicreadingsbydrkelly.webs.com/

What We'll Cover

WHAT ARE CHAKRAS?

Chakra Assessment Quiz

The Seven Chakras

Chakra Clearing and Balancing

Chakra Scan and Strengthening

Contact Me/Book a Reading

What Are Chakras?

NOT EVERYONE BELIEVES in the presence of chakras, but if you think of them as energy centers within your body, like smaller auras, it's easier to imagine. These centers are conduits for universal energy, linking your consciousness and higher mind.

Think of yourself as a lot of energy contained in a flesh and blood vessel. If you want to strengthen your psychic abilities and be healthier all around, you need to strengthen your energy centers. When your chakras are balanced you'll feel more at peace, have a clearer mind, feel more connected to Spirit, will be healthier and happier, and your intuition will be heightened.

"Chakra" is a Sanskrit word meaning wheel or vortex, and refers to the many energy centers of your body. These energy centers are not visible to the human eye, though intuitive people are able to see chakras in their mind's eye or sense them.

There are hundreds of chakras in the human body, but we only need to focus on the seven main chakras that line up from the base of the spine to the top of the head. Each chakra has a specific color associated with it and represents certain aspects of your physical, emotional, and spiritual body. The chakras are made of pure energy and each one spins with its own unique vibration, gathering and releasing energy as they turn.

Your physical health can play a huge role in your spiritual health and vice versa. If one or more of your chakras are out of balance, then it will affect your spiritual energy. Once this is out of whack a long list of ailments—mental, physical, emotional and spiritual—can crop up.

Since this is a book about spiritual power, healing, and intuitive living, we'll focus on what each of these chakras represents, problems that may arise, and how to correct them so you'll be more in harmony on all levels.

Before we get in deeper, let's take a chakra assessment quiz, so you can get an idea of which of your chakras need healing or an energy boost. All you need to do is answer yes or no to each question below and see which chakra(s) need extra care and attention right now. I recommend taking this quiz every six months or so just to see how you're doing.

Chakra Assessment

FIRST CHAKRA, ROOT Chakra:

- Do you dislike change and crave stability and security?

- Do you have various fears or phobias?

- Do you have trouble trusting people?

- Do you have arthritis, joint pain, or bone issues?

- Do you have sensitive skin, rashes, eczema, psoriasis, or dermatitis?

- Do you have an autoimmune disorder?

- Do you suffer from any allergies; whether seasonal, environmental, or food related?

Second Chakra, Sacral Chakra:

- Do you suffer from chronic lower back pain?

- Do you have issues with fertility, PMS, or menopause?

- Do you have mood swings or frequent depression?

- Do you suffer from chronic fatigue, adrenal burnout, or low energy?

- Do you suffer from chronic guilt or worry?

- Do you find it hard to tell others no and set personal boundaries?

- Do you have any sexual dysfunctions or addictions?

Third Chakra, Solar Plexus Chakra:

- Do you have any addictions like alcohol, food, shopping, porn, or gambling?

- Do you constantly struggle with your weight?

- Do you have chronic constipation, gas, bloating, or digestive issues?

- Do you have diabetes or hypoglycemia?

- Do you have gallstones, gallbladder pain, or recurring gallbladder attacks?

- Do you feel you're frequently on-guard, hypervigilant, easy to anger or upset?

- Do you feel you're a nervous or jumpy person?

Fourth Chakra, Heart Chakra:

- Do you have a history of trauma, neglect, or abuse?

- Do you put everyone's health and happiness before your own?

- Do you find it hard to let people get close to you, so you put up walls to stay safe?

- Do you suffer from fibromyalgia, chronic sore or weak muscles, or any breast issues?

- Do you have heart issues or circulation problems?

- Do you feel unworthy of love, fear rejection, or love too much too soon?

- Do you ignore or mistrust your own intuition when it comes to others?

Fifth Chakra, Throat Chakra:

- Do you have trouble expressing your feelings or speaking up for yourself?

- Do you have chronic sore throats, laryngitis, strep throat, or dry throat?

- Do you have a thyroid issue: hypothyroidism, hyperthyroid, or Hashimoto's disease?

- Do you have chronic gum or dental problems, grind your teeth, or have jaw pain?

- Do you talk more than you listen?

- Do you freeze up if you have to talk in front of a group?

- Do you find that you're introverted, shy, or timid?

Sixth Chakra, Third Eye Chakra:

- Do you suffer from migraines, chronic headaches, or sinus problems?

- Do you have vision problems or other eye issues?

- Do you suffer from anxiety, depression, or being overly sensitive?

- Do you overanalyze things or tend to be too logical?

- Do you have a bad memory, often forgetting things or people's names?

- Do you have frequent nightmares?

- Do you daydream or fantasize a lot?

Seventh Chakra, Crown Chakra:

- Do you have a short attention span?

- Do you often feel dizzy, lightheaded, or feel disconnected from reality?

- Do you sometimes feel you don't belong?

- Do you have trouble making decisions?

- Do you find it difficult to believe in or find your spirituality?

- Do you often feel lost or alone?

- Do you constantly feel frustrated and dissatisfied?

After reading over these questions I'm sure you said yes to at least a few or many. Everyone has strengths and weaknesses, wounds and traumas.

Don't feel defeated if you experience a lot of the above issues. Knowledge is power and knowing where you have energy blockages can point you in the direction to finally transform your mind, body, and soul. Soon you'll be living life on your own terms, in alignment with your higher self, and feeling happier and healthier than you can probably ever remember being.

The Seven Chakras

EACH CHAKRA HAS ITS own vibrational frequency that's depicted through a specific chakra color. They also govern specific functions that help make you who you are as both a human being and spiritual being.

As you read over the information about each chakra, you might instantly see which of your energy centers is blocked and has been causing your problems. This will be the first chakra you'll want to work on. However, all chakras are interwoven, and working with one will help all the others to some extent.

Root Chakra – Survival, Trust, Safety, Family Loyalty

Your first chakra is called the root chakra and is located at the base of your spine. It vibrates at the rate of the color red and is associated with survival and self-preservation. It's your foundation chakra that enables you to get your basic needs met while here on Earth such as food, shelter, and water.

The developmental stage of this chakra is from conception through your first 12 months of life. This is where you start working on your physical identity. The greatest challenge related to this chakra is that of fear. Having your basic needs met during your first year of life is important to feeling safe and learning to trust others.

The physical association is the bones, teeth, large intestine, kidneys, and blood.

CHAKRA ENERGY

Sacral Chakra – Creativity, Sexuality, Relationships, Pleasure

The second chakra is located just below your navel. It vibrates at the rate of the color orange and is associated with your ability to be creative, reproduction, and fertility—which includes being fertile with ideas, abundance, etc.

The basic need of this chakra is related to the emotions. The developmental stage for the sacral chakra is six months to two years of age. Since this is the "pleasure" chakra, it's where we begin to explore our wants and feelings. We need to experience an emotional connection to our world and others. The greatest challenge related to this chakra is feelings of guilt.

The physical association is the uterus, genitals, kidney, and bladder.

Solar Plexus Chakra – Confidence, Personal Power, Personality, Self-Control

Located below the ribs is the third chakra or the solar plexus chakra. This chakra vibrates at the rate of the color yellow and is your source of inner power and self-worth.

The developmental state is between the ages of 18 months to four years. This is when we start working on our ego identity and interacting with others. The greatest challenge faced when this chakra is out of balance or blocked is feelings of shame.

The physical association is the digestive system, liver, and gallbladder.

Heart Chakra – Love, Compassion, Respect

The heart chakra is the fourth chakra and is considered the bridge between the lower three chakras (earth) and the upper 3 chakras (spirit). It's located directly in the center of your chest and vibrates at the rate of the color green. This chakra relates to love—including self-love—and compassion.

We begin developing this chakra between that ages of three to seven years where we start venturing outside of ourselves more, seeking social identity. The challenge associated with the heart chakra is grief. From three to seven is when we typically experience our first loss of someone or something dear to us. Although we might not be able to fully understand our feelings, the grief is deeply felt.

The physical association is anything to do with the heart, lungs, circulatory system, arms, and hands.

Throat Chakra – Self-expression, Communication, Truth

The fifth chakra is located in the throat and vibrates at the rate of the color blue. It relates to the right to express your truth, and finding your creative identity. The developmental stage for this chakra is between the ages of seven to twelve years. Chronic throat issues is a clear indication that you've been holding back from expressing your true emotions, especially those of sadness and anger.

The greatest challenge related to the throat chakra is communication. That's not to say that you should go around being blunt and saying whatever's on your mind. There's a good balance between honest self-expression and having respect for others' feelings.

The physical association is the throat, ears, mouth, shoulders, and neck

Third Eye Chakra – Self-Reflection, Spiritual Contemplation, Access to Higher Guidance

Residing in the forehead is the sixth chakra or the third-eye chakra, also called the brow chakra. It vibrates at the rate of the color indigo and is associated with your mind and intuitive abilities.

This chakra develops in adolescence and its main function is imagination and intuition. The greatest challenge associate with the third-eye is differentiating illusion from spiritual and psychic truth.

When you're first venturing into the spiritual world it can get overwhelming and hard to figure out what's real and what's your imagination. I always say that intuition and imagination are closely related—you can't tap into one without the other. Over time you'll discover your own truth, yet will continue to grow.

The physical association are the eyes, the base of the skull, and the forehead.

Crown Chakra – Deep Understanding, Inner Wisdom, Enlightenment, Higher-Self

This is the seventh chakra and is located at the top of the head. It vibrates at the rate of the color violet or white and develops throughout life. This chakra deals with your right to know and learn, and brings you awareness and understanding at a higher level.

The greatest challenge people face when this chakra is blocked or out of balance is attachment issues. Usually, this comes in the form of material attachments. More stuff never makes us happy since true joy is created within ourselves. Developing this chakra will help you live in harmony with your soul and find your life purpose.

The physical association is the nervous system and cerebral cortex.

Now that we've looked at each individual chakra, let's get to some exercises that will help you clear and balance any of your energy centers.

Chakra Clearing and Balancing

AS WE'VE TALKED ABOUT, when all your chakras are gently spinning or seem bright, you can then say your chakra system is completely balanced. These days it's almost impossible to be in total balance at all times. Everything that has happened to you in life—at birth, during your childhood, teenage years, even five minutes ago—influences your chakra energy.

As you go through various problems or situations in life, one or more of your chakras can get out of balance, closed off, or too open. When this happens, it can affect your mental, emotional, physical, and/or spiritual self.

Every habit you have, every feeling, thought, fear, belief, worry, desire, or dream can be found in your chakras. These energy centers hold on to all your energy—the good and the bad. If you encounter a situation or person who negatively affects your life in some way, it can be stored in one or more of your chakras unless you work through it and heal it.

Over time, I'm sure you can see how things can pile up in your chakras and throw them off balance. No wonder people have so many problems in their lives they can't seem to let go of!

Cleansing, strengthening and balancing your chakras is very beneficial for your body, mind, and spirit. It helps the aura's energy to stay as pure as possible and can increase your intuitive abilities.

I do this at least once a week to help raise my energy, strengthen my psychic gifts and eliminate any negative build-up in my chakras. You can repeat the following exercise daily or weekly and work on all your chakras or focus only on the chakra(s) you feel are most out of balance.

Don't be surprised if you can't cleanse them the very first time. This exercise takes practice and you may have a lot of junk built up in your chakras. After you get used to doing this meditation it should only take about ten minutes.

Chakra Scan and Strengthening

TO BEGIN, GO TO A QUIET place, light some incense and/or a candle, and put on some soothing music if you'd like. Sit in a chair or on your bed. Try not to lie down since you may end up falling asleep.

Take a deep breath through your nose as you count to five, hold it for a count of five, then exhale slowly through your mouth to a count of ten. (Imagine blowing on a spoonful of hot soup as you blow out.)

As you continue to breathe like this 5-10 more times, consciously relax all the muscles in your body. What I do is the first time I breathe in then out I focus on my head and shoulders. With the next breath I focus on my chest and arms. The next breath relaxes my back and waist. The fourth breath relaxes my hips and pelvis. The fifth breath relaxes my thighs and knees. The sixth breath relaxes my calves and feet. The last four breaths are spent letting my mind go and just relaxing my body as a whole.

By now you should feel relaxed and at peace. If thoughts or images wander into your mind just let them pass through. If you need to, go back over the breathing and relaxation steps until you ultimately feel relaxed.

Root Chakra

Imagine a bright red ball floating inside your body at the base of your spine. This signifies your root chakra, which corresponds to survival, trust, and safety.

As you visualize this ball see if you can detect any dark or cold spots, or if the ball of light seems too bright or too dim. Just sense this. If anything seems off about this chakra imagine your guides or the Universe sending healing energy to this chakra so that it becomes a warm, bright red color.

As you focus on this you may feel a tingling sensation, warmth, or a surge of energy. This lets you know that your chakra is being cleansed and healed. Even if you don't feel anything right away, simply move on to the next part of the exercise.

While you do the visualization repeat this affirmation either out loud or in your mind:

"I am safe and secure at all times. I am responsible for the quality of my life. I am free to make changes."

Sacral Chakra

As you do your visualization exercise, move your attention upward about three inches and imagine an orange ball floating inside you, around the area of your navel. This is your sacral chakra, which is the regulator of your creativity, sexuality, relationships, and pleasure. Scan this chakra for any areas of darkness, coldness, or anything that seems off.

Breathe in deeply to bring more light and energy into this chakra and to cleanse away all negativity. After a few breaths imagine that this chakra is glowing a bright and beautiful color of orange.

While you do the visualization repeat this affirmation either out loud or in your mind:

"I am good enough to have what I want. I release my negative thoughts and attitudes. I give myself permission to experience pleasure."

Solar Plexus Chakra

Concentrate now on the area about three inches above your navel, which is where your solar plexus chakra is. This is the area where you usually feel those gut instincts. The solar plexus chakra is affected by your beliefs concerning personal power and self-control. You also may not be able to tune into your intuition properly when this chakra is off.

Imagine a yellow ball glowing brightly inside you and check to see if there are any holes or dark areas on your solar plexus chakra. If you see or sense that anything is off in this area, breathe in deeply and ask your guides or the Universe to send healing energy until the chakra becomes a brilliant light-yellow color.

While you do the visualization repeat this affirmation either out loud or in your mind:

"I love and respect myself at all time. I learn from everything I do. I trust my instincts."

Heart Chakra

As you continue the exercise, move your attention to your heart area and visualize or feel a soothing green ball of light in your chest. This is your heart chakra, the center of your loving energy.

Scan your heart chakra and look for any areas of darkness, holes, or anything that seems off about it. As you did before, breathe in through your nose while imagining that your guides or the Universe are sending you healing and cleansing light. Fill up your heart chakra with this loving light and feel it warming your chest area. Keep breathing until the green light in your chakra is completely clean and vibrant.

While you do the visualization repeat this affirmation either out loud or in your mind:

"I open myself to love and follow the path of the heart. I am loved, and I love others unconditionally."

Throat Chakra

Now you'll concentrate on your throat chakra as you imagine a ball of beautiful blue light in this area. This chakra dictates the clarity of all your communications: truthfully speaking your mind and feelings, and interacting with others on a verbal level.

Mentally scan your throat chakra, looking for or feeling for dark or muddy areas. Just as you did before, breathe slowly and deeply through your nose while visualizing your guides or the Universe sending a warm and healing light that will cleanse this chakra. As you breathe out again, see or sense your chakra as being bright and clean.

While you do the visualization repeat this affirmation either out loud or in your mind:

"I am safe to express myself to others as long as my words are truthful, loving, and helpful. I release all fear and doubts that block my creativity."

Third Eye Chakra

Now move your attention to your forehead, right where your third eye would be. This chakra is an indigo color and is the center of your sixth sense or psychic abilities. Breathe in and ask your guides to cleanse and strengthen this chakra and imagine the ball of light there as a vibrant indigo color completely cleansed of any darkness or problems.

While focusing on this chakra you may see an eye on the inside of your forehead, if so, you're getting a glimpse of your third eye. If the eye seems closed, mentally ask it to open. Some people become shaken or excited to actually see their own third eye open.

Since this is the seat of your higher self, feel free to ask your third eye for any guidance or any questions you may need answers to and take notes afterward. As you get more accustomed to using your third eye you'll receive telepathic messages from your higher self on a regular basis.

While you do the visualization repeat this affirmation either out loud or in your mind:

"It is safe for me to see the truth in everything and everyone."

Crown Chakra

Now you'll move on to the crown chakra, which is the last one. You can focus your attention directly on the top of your head or three inches above it; whichever feels more natural to you.

This chakra allows you to contact your guides and the wisdom of the Universe. It's white, which is the entire color spectrum.

Breathe in and ask your guides to send pure, clean energy to this chakra, to strengthen it and open it so that you can communicate with them at any time. Continue your deep breathing exercise until you feel that this last chakra is vibrant and balanced.

While you do the visualization repeat this affirmation either out loud or in your mind:

"I am always protected and guided as I take the next step in my life. I am open to the goodness and abundance of the Universe."

Ending the Meditation

To end the chakra meditation session, simply thank your guides for healing, cleansing, and balancing your chakras and for protecting you. Take one last deep breath in for a count of five, hold for five, and then let it out quickly through your mouth like blowing out a candle. This forces any lingering negativity to be released. Slowly open your eyes and stretch a bit before standing since you may feel a bit dizzy. Once you stand up, walk around a little and stretch again.

This exercise is excellent for helping you to cleanse, heal, balance and strengthen your chakras. When each of your chakras, those mini-aura centers, are bright and spinning correctly, your life will be better in all areas.

CHAKRA ENERGY

After the Meditation

Once you finish this meditation you may feel totally energized or very peaceful and relaxed. You should be able to think more clearly and have more focus. In time you may find that your health improves, your energy levels are higher, and you grow mentally, physically, emotionally, and spiritually.

When I began this meditation practice I noticed big differences in my outlook on life, my energy levels, and the fact that more beneficial opportunities and people started coming my way. When life stops moving forward or negative things begin to happen I do this meditation exercise and things clear up right away.

Keep Practicing

Now that you've gotten an overview of some ways to cleanse, heal and balance your chakras, the key is to keep practicing. The worst thing you can do is become discouraged and give up. Always keep practicing since we are all lifelong students. There are no true masters, only those who are farther ahead on the spiritual path.

Contact Me/Book A Reading

WHETHER YOUR PROBLEMS or concerns are in the areas of love, finances, family, career, health, education, or your path in life, I offer professional psychic counseling, caring guidance, and solutions that work!

I use no tools. Instead, I'll connect directly with your higher self and your spirit guides to help you through any situation and achieve the best possible results. No problem is too big or too small, and your questions will be answered in detail.

I'll let you know absolutely everything that comes through in the reading which typically includes past, present, and future energies, guidance, time frames and predictions. Your guides may also include information on an important past life, aura energy, soul symbols, and more. Each reading is in-depth, filled with positive energy and guidance, and includes one free clarification email.

All readings are done via email. By offering my readings through email you'll be able to save your reading and go back to it again and again for guidance.

I look forward to reading for you!

Check out my readings, books, blog posts, and more on my website:

PsychicReadingsByDrKelly.webs.com[1]

Or email me directly at: DrKellyPsychicCounselor@gmail.com

---

1. http://psychicreadingsbydrkelly.webs.com/psychic-readings

Made in the USA
Columbia, SC
29 January 2022